This Planner Belongs To:

_____

A Look At My Assets & Liabilities

YEARLY FINANCIAL *Goals*

THIS YEAR *my primary goals are*

JAN

FEB

MAR

APR

MAY

JUN

JUL

AUG

SEP

OCT

NOV

DEC

BALANCE Sheet

DATE:

CREDIT SCORE:

NET WORTH:

FINANCIALS

LIABILITIES: **ASSETS:**

	ASSETS	AMOUNT		LIABILITIES	AMOUNT
CASH			**DEBTS**		
	SUBTOTAL:			**SUBTOTAL:**	
INVESTMENTS			**LOANS**		
	SUBTOTAL:			**SUBTOTAL:**	
REAL ESTATE			**MORTGAGE**		
	SUBTOTAL:			**SUBTOTAL:**	
OTHER			**OTHER**		
	SUBTOTAL:			**SUBTOTAL:**	

DEBT REPAYMENT *Plan*

ACCOUNT:

PRIORITY#

COMPANY:

CREDIT TYPE:

CREDIT LIMIT:

GOAL PAYOFF DATE

WEBSITE URL:

USERNAME: PASSWORD:

STARTING BALANCE:

INTEREST ACCRUED: DUE DATE:

PAYMENT DATE	PAYMENT AMOUNT	CURRENT BALANCE

DEBT REPAYMENT *Plan*

ACCOUNT:

PRIORITY#

COMPANY:

CREDIT TYPE:

CREDIT LIMIT:

WEBSITE URL:

USERNAME: PASSWORD:

STARTING BALANCE:

INTEREST ACCRUED: DUE DATE:

GOAL PAYOFF DATE

PAYMENT DATE	PAYMENT AMOUNT	CURRENT BALANCE

ACCOUNT Tracker

ACCOUNT #1

FINANCIAL INSTITUTION:

ACCOUNT #:

NAME ON ACCOUNT:

ACCOUNT TYPE:

CARD NUMBER:

ROUTING/TRANSIT #:

OTHER:

NOTES

ACCOUNT #2

FINANCIAL INSTITUTION:

ACCOUNT #:

NAME ON ACCOUNT:

ACCOUNT TYPE:

CARD NUMBER:

ROUTING/TRANSIT #:

OTHER:

NOTES

ACCOUNT #3

FINANCIAL INSTITUTION:

ACCOUNT #:

NAME ON ACCOUNT:

ACCOUNT TYPE:

CARD NUMBER:

ROUTING/TRANSIT #:

OTHER:

NOTES

AUTO REPAIR *Tracker*

CAR MAKE: **YEAR:**

CAR MODEL: **VIN #:**

DATE	REPAIR	COST

HOME REPAIR Tracker

YEAR:

DATE	REPAIR	COST

MY TRAVEL Budget

BUDGET BREAKDOWN:

PLANE TICKETS:

TRANSPORTATION:

LODGING:

FOOD/SHOPPING:

TRAVEL NOTES:

GOAL PAYOFF DATE

TOTALS:

TOTAL COST OF TRIP: AMOUNT TO RAISE:

PAYMENT DATE	PAYMENT AMOUNT	CURRENT BALANCE

TRAVEL *Contacts*

LOCATION:

HOTEL:

ADDRESS #:   WEBSITE URL:
PHONE#:   AMOUNT PER NIGHT::

RESERVATION INFORMATION: **DUE DATE:**   **ROOM DETAILS:**

BILL TOTAL:

HOTEL:

ACCOUNT #:   WEBSITE URL:
PHONE#:   AMOUNT PER NIGHT::

RESERVATION INFORMATION: **DUE DATE:**   **ROOM DETAILS:**

BILL TOTAL:

HOTEL:

ACCOUNT #:   WEBSITE URL:
PHONE#:   AMOUNT PER NIGHT:

RESERVATION INFORMATION: **DUE DATE:**   **ROOM DETAILS:**

BILL TOTAL:

NOTES

TRAVEL *Contacts*

LOCATION:

CAR RENTAL:

ADDRESS #: WEBSITE URL:
PHONE#: AMOUNT PER NIGHT::

RESERVATION INFORMATION: **DUE DATE:** **CAR DETAILS:**

BILL TOTAL:

CAR RENTAL:

ACCOUNT #: WEBSITE URL:
PHONE#: AMOUNT PER NIGHT::

RESERVATION INFORMATION: **DUE DATE:** **CAR DETAILS:**

BILL TOTAL:

TRAIN PASS:

ACCOUNT #: WEBSITE URL:
PHONE#: AMOUNT PER NIGHT:

RESERVATION INFORMATION: **DUE DATE:** **PASS DETAILS:**

BILL TOTAL:

NOTES

TRAVEL *Contacts*

LOCATION:

TRAIN PASS:

ADDRESS #:   WEBSITE URL:

PHONE#:   AMOUNT PER NIGHT::

RESERVATION INFORMATION: **DUE DATE:**   **TRAIN DETAILS:**

BILL TOTAL:

AIRPLANE TICKETS:

AIRLINE: WEBSITE URL:

PHONE #:   AMOUNT PER SEAT::

RESERVATION INFORMATION: **DUE DATE:**   **FLIGHT DETAILS:**

BILL TOTAL:

EVENT TICKETS:

EVENT: WEBSITE URL:

PHONE#:   AMOUNT PER TICKET

RESERVATION INFORMATION: **DUE DATE:**   **EVENT DETAILS:**

BILL TOTAL:

NOTES

Planning My Monthly Budget

RECURRING Bills

FREQUENCY:

COMPANY:

ACCOUNT #:   WEBSITE URL:

PHONE #:   BILL DUE DATE:

ONLINE ACCOUNT INFORMATION: **USERNAME**   **PASSWORD**

BILL TOTAL:

COMPANY:

ACCOUNT #:   WEBSITE URL:

PHONE #:   BILL DUE DATE:

ONLINE ACCOUNT INFORMATION: **USERNAME**   **PASSWORD**

BILL TOTAL:

COMPANY:

ACCOUNT #:   WEBSITE URL:

PHONE #:   BILL DUE DATE:

ONLINE ACCOUNT INFORMATION: **USERNAME**   **PASSWORD**

BILL TOTAL:

NOTES

RECURRING Bills

FREQUENCY:

COMPANY:

ACCOUNT #:   WEBSITE URL:

PHONE#:   BILL DUE DATE:

ONLINE ACCOUNT INFORMATION: **USERNAME**   **PASSWORD**

BILL TOTAL:

COMPANY:

ACCOUNT #:   WEBSITE URL:

PHONE#:   BILL DUE DATE:

ONLINE ACCOUNT INFORMATION: **USERNAME**   **PASSWORD**

BILL TOTAL:

COMPANY:

ACCOUNT #:   WEBSITE URL:

PHONE#:   BILL DUE DATE:

ONLINE ACCOUNT INFORMATION: **USERNAME**   **PASSWORD**

BILL TOTAL:

NOTES

RECURRING Bills

FREQUENCY:

COMPANY:

ACCOUNT #:   WEBSITE URL:
PHONE#:   BILL DUE DATE:

ONLINE ACCOUNT INFORMATION: **USERNAME**   **PASSWORD**

BILL TOTAL:

COMPANY:

ACCOUNT #:   WEBSITE URL:
PHONE#:   BILL DUE DATE:

ONLINE ACCOUNT INFORMATION: **USERNAME**   **PASSWORD**

BILL TOTAL:

COMPANY:

ACCOUNT #:   WEBSITE URL:
PHONE#:   BILL DUE DATE:

ONLINE ACCOUNT INFORMATION: **USERNAME**   **PASSWORD**

BILL TOTAL:

NOTES

RECURRING Bills

FREQUENCY:

COMPANY:

ACCOUNT #:   WEBSITE URL:

PHONE#:   BILL DUE DATE:

ONLINE ACCOUNT INFORMATION: **USERNAME**   **PASSWORD**

BILL TOTAL:

COMPANY:

ACCOUNT #:   WEBSITE URL:

PHONE#:   BILL DUE DATE:

ONLINE ACCOUNT INFORMATION: **USERNAME**   **PASSWORD**

BILL TOTAL:

COMPANY:

ACCOUNT #:   WEBSITE URL:

PHONE#:   BILL DUE DATE:

ONLINE ACCOUNT INFORMATION: **USERNAME**   **PASSWORD**

BILL TOTAL:

NOTES

INCOME *Tracker*
- MONTHLY -

SOURCE	AMOUNT	M	T	W	T	F	S	S

MONTHLY Budget

MONTHLY INCOME:	BUDGETED:	ACTUAL COST:	DIFFERENCE:

Household Utilities/Expenses

SUBTOTAL:		**% OF INCOME:**	

Debt/Payments/Travel Budget

SUBTOTAL:		**% OF INCOME:**	

Personal/Other

SUBTOTAL:		**% OF INCOME:**	

MONTHLY EXPENSE *Tracker*

MONTH:

GROCERIES

DATE	ITEM	AMOUNT

HOME

DATE	ITEM	AMOUNT

PERSONAL

DATE	ITEM	AMOUNT

ACTIVITIES

DATE	ITEM	AMOUNT

RECREATION

DATE	ITEM	AMOUNT

MISC

DATE	ITEM	AMOUNT

Goal Setting & Daily Spending Actuals

MONTH 1

Date:_____

INCOME *Tracker*
- MONTHLY -

SOURCE	AMOUNT	M	T	W	T	F	S	S

ONE-TIME Bills

MONTH:

COMPANY:

ACCOUNT #:　　　　　　　　　　　　　WEBSITE URL:
PHONE #:　　　　　　　　　　　　　　BILL DUE DATE:

ONLINE ACCOUNT INFORMATION:　　　**USERNAME**　　**PASSWORD**

BILL TOTAL:

COMPANY:

ACCOUNT #:　　　　　　　　　　　　　WEBSITE URL:
PHONE #:　　　　　　　　　　　　　　BILL DUE DATE:

ONLINE ACCOUNT INFORMATION:　　　**USERNAME**　　**PASSWORD**

BILL TOTAL:

COMPANY:

ACCOUNT #:　　　　　　　　　　　　　WEBSITE URL:
PHONE #:　　　　　　　　　　　　　　BILL DUE DATE:

ONLINE ACCOUNT INFORMATION:　　　**USERNAME**　　**PASSWORD**

BILL TOTAL:

NOTES

ONE-TIME *Bills*

MONTH:

COMPANY:

ACCOUNT #: WEBSITE URL:
PHONE #: BILL DUE DATE:

ONLINE ACCOUNT INFORMATION: **USERNAME** **PASSWORD**

BILL TOTAL:

COMPANY:

ACCOUNT #: WEBSITE URL:
PHONE #: BILL DUE DATE:

ONLINE ACCOUNT INFORMATION: **USERNAME** **PASSWORD**

BILL TOTAL:

COMPANY:

ACCOUNT #: WEBSITE URL:
PHONE #: BILL DUE DATE:

ONLINE ACCOUNT INFORMATION: **USERNAME** **PASSWORD**

BILL TOTAL:

NOTES

WEEKLY EXPENSE *Tracker*

DATES:

DESCRIPTION	CATEGORY	COST	NEED	WANT

DAILY LIFE *Planner*

DATES:

TODAY, *my primary goals are*

- **MOR**
- **AFT**
- **EVE**

TODAY, *my primary goals are*

- **MOR**
- **AFT**
- **EVE**

TODAY, *my primary goals are*

- **MOR**
- **AFT**
- **EVE**

DAILY LIFE *Planner*

DATES:

TODAY, *my primary goals are*

MOR
_____
_____
_____

AFT
_____
_____
_____

EVE
_____
_____
_____

TODAY, *my primary goals are*

MOR
_____
_____
_____

AFT
_____
_____
_____

EVE
_____
_____
_____

TODAY, *my primary goals are*

MOR
_____
_____
_____

AFT
_____
_____
_____

EVE
_____
_____
_____

DAILY LIFE *Planner*

DATES:

TODAY, *my primary goals are*

MOR

_____
_____
_____

AFT

_____
_____
_____

EVE

_____
_____
_____

NOTES:

WEEKLY EXPENSE *Tracker*

DATES:

DESCRIPTION	CATEGORY	COST	NEED	WANT

DAILY LIFE *Planner*

DATES:

TODAY, *my primary goals are*

MOR

AFT

EVE

TODAY, *my primary goals are*

MOR

AFT

EVE

TODAY, *my primary goals are*

MOR

AFT

EVE

DAILY LIFE *Planner*

DATES:

TODAY, *my primary goals are*

(**MOR**)   (**AFT**)   (**EVE**)

_____ _____ _____
_____ _____ _____
_____ _____ _____

TODAY, *my primary goals are*

(**MOR**)   (**AFT**)   (**EVE**)

_____ _____ _____
_____ _____ _____
_____ _____ _____

TODAY, *my primary goals are*

(**MOR**)   (**AFT**)   (**EVE**)

_____ _____ _____
_____ _____ _____
_____ _____ _____

DAILY LIFE *Planner*

DATES:

TODAY, *my primary goals are*

MOR

AFT

EVE

NOTES:

WEEKLY EXPENSE *Tracker*

DATES:

DESCRIPTION	CATEGORY	COST	NEED	WANT

DAILY LIFE *Planner*

DATES:

TODAY, *my primary goals are*

MOR

AFT

EVE

TODAY, *my primary goals are*

MOR

AFT

EVE

TODAY, *my primary goals are*

MOR

AFT

EVE

DAILY LIFE *Planner*

DATES:

TODAY, *my primary goals are*

| MOR | AFT | EVE |

TODAY, *my primary goals are*

| MOR | AFT | EVE |

TODAY, *my primary goals are*

| MOR | AFT | EVE |

DAILY LIFE *Planner*

DATES:

TODAY, *my primary goals are*

MOR

AFT

EVE

NOTES:

WEEKLY EXPENSE *Tracker*

DATES:

DESCRIPTION	CATEGORY	COST	NEED	WANT

DAILY LIFE *Planner*

DATES:

TODAY, *my primary goals are*

- **MOR**
- **AFT**
- **EVE**

TODAY, *my primary goals are*

- **MOR**
- **AFT**
- **EVE**

TODAY, *my primary goals are*

- **MOR**
- **AFT**
- **EVE**

DAILY LIFE *Planner*

DATES:

TODAY, *my primary goals are*

MOR
_____
_____
_____

AFT
_____
_____
_____

EVE
_____
_____
_____

TODAY, *my primary goals are*

MOR
_____
_____
_____

AFT
_____
_____
_____

EVE
_____
_____
_____

TODAY, *my primary goals are*

MOR
_____
_____
_____

AFT
_____
_____
_____

EVE
_____
_____
_____

DAILY LIFE *Planner*

DATES:

TODAY, *my primary goals are*

MOR

_____
_____
_____

AFT

_____
_____
_____

EVE

_____
_____
_____

NOTES:

FINANCIAL Journal

MONTH 2

Date:_____

INCOME Tracker
- MONTHLY -

SOURCE	AMOUNT	M	T	W	T	F	S	S

ONE-TIME *Bills*

MONTH:

COMPANY:

ACCOUNT #:

WEBSITE URL:

PHONE#:

BILL DUE DATE:

ONLINE ACCOUNT INFORMATION: **USERNAME**   **PASSWORD**

BILL TOTAL:

COMPANY:

ACCOUNT #:

WEBSITE URL:

PHONE#:

BILL DUE DATE:

ONLINE ACCOUNT INFORMATION: **USERNAME**   **PASSWORD**

BILL TOTAL:

COMPANY:

ACCOUNT #:

WEBSITE URL:

PHONE#:

BILL DUE DATE:

ONLINE ACCOUNT INFORMATION: **USERNAME**   **PASSWORD**

BILL TOTAL:

NOTES

ONE-TIME *Bills*

MONTH:

COMPANY:

ACCOUNT #:   WEBSITE URL:

PHONE #:   BILL DUE DATE:

ONLINE ACCOUNT INFORMATION: **USERNAME**   **PASSWORD**

BILL TOTAL:

COMPANY:

ACCOUNT #:   WEBSITE URL:

PHONE #:   BILL DUE DATE:

ONLINE ACCOUNT INFORMATION: **USERNAME**   **PASSWORD**

BILL TOTAL:

COMPANY:

ACCOUNT #:   WEBSITE URL:

PHONE #:   BILL DUE DATE:

ONLINE ACCOUNT INFORMATION: **USERNAME**   **PASSWORD**

BILL TOTAL:

NOTES

WEEKLY EXPENSE *Tracker*

DATES:

DESCRIPTION	CATEGORY	COST	NEED	WANT

DAILY LIFE *Planner*

DATES:

TODAY, *my primary goals are*

MOR
_____
_____
_____
_____

AFT
_____
_____
_____
_____

EVE
_____
_____
_____
_____

TODAY, *my primary goals are*

MOR
_____
_____
_____
_____

AFT
_____
_____
_____
_____

EVE
_____
_____
_____
_____

TODAY, *my primary goals are*

MOR
_____
_____
_____
_____

AFT
_____
_____
_____
_____

EVE
_____
_____
_____
_____

DAILY LIFE *Planner*

DATES:

TODAY, *my primary goals are*

MOR

AFT

EVE

TODAY, *my primary goals are*

MOR

AFT

EVE

TODAY, *my primary goals are*

MOR

AFT

EVE

DAILY LIFE *Planner*

DATES:

TODAY, *my primary goals are*

MOR

****
****
****

AFT

****
****
****

EVE

****
****
****

NOTES:

WEEKLY EXPENSE *Tracker*

DATES:

DESCRIPTION	CATEGORY	COST	NEED	WANT

DAILY LIFE *Planner*

DATES:

TODAY, *my primary goals are*

MOR
....
....
....

AFT
....
....
....

EVE
....
....
....

TODAY, *my primary goals are*

MOR
....
....
....

AFT
....
....
....

EVE
....
....
....

TODAY, *my primary goals are*

MOR
....
....
....

AFT
....
....
....

EVE
....
....
....

DAILY LIFE *Planner*

DATES:

TODAY, *my primary goals are*

MOR

AFT

EVE

TODAY, *my primary goals are*

MOR

AFT

EVE

TODAY, *my primary goals are*

MOR

AFT

EVE

DAILY LIFE *Planner*

DATES:

TODAY, *my primary goals are*

MOR

AFT

EVE

NOTES:

WEEKLY EXPENSE *Tracker*

DATES:

DESCRIPTION	CATEGORY	COST	NEED	WANT

DAILY LIFE *Planner*

DATES:

TODAY, *my primary goals are*

MOR
_____
_____
_____

AFT
_____
_____
_____

EVE
_____
_____
_____

TODAY, *my primary goals are*

MOR
_____
_____
_____

AFT
_____
_____
_____

EVE
_____
_____
_____

TODAY, *my primary goals are*

MOR
_____
_____
_____

AFT
_____
_____
_____

EVE
_____
_____
_____

DAILY LIFE *Planner*

DATES:

TODAY, *my primary goals are*

MOR   **AFT**   **EVE**

_____   _____   _____
_____   _____   _____
_____   _____   _____

TODAY, *my primary goals are*

MOR   **AFT**   **EVE**

_____   _____   _____
_____   _____   _____
_____   _____   _____

TODAY, *my primary goals are*

MOR   **AFT**   **EVE**

_____   _____   _____
_____   _____   _____
_____   _____   _____

DAILY LIFE *Planner*

DATES:

TODAY, *my primary goals are*

MOR
_____
_____
_____

AFT
_____
_____
_____

EVE
_____
_____
_____

NOTES:

WEEKLY EXPENSE *Tracker*

DATES:

DESCRIPTION	CATEGORY	COST	NEED	WANT

DAILY LIFE *Planner*

DATES:

TODAY, *my primary goals are*

MOR

....
....
....
....

AFT

....
....
....
....

EVE

....
....
....
....

TODAY, *my primary goals are*

MOR

....
....
....
....

AFT

....
....
....
....

EVE

....
....
....
....

TODAY, *my primary goals are*

MOR

....
....
....
....

AFT

....
....
....
....

EVE

....
....
....
....

DAILY LIFE *Planner*

DATES:

TODAY, *my primary goals are*

MOR

AFT

EVE

TODAY, *my primary goals are*

MOR

AFT

EVE

TODAY, *my primary goals are*

MOR

AFT

EVE

DAILY LIFE *Planner*

DATES:

TODAY, *my primary goals are*

MOR

AFT

EVE

NOTES:

FINANCIAL Journal

MONTH 3

Date:_____

INCOME *Tracker*
- MONTHLY -

SOURCE	AMOUNT	M	T	W	T	F	S	S

ONE-TIME Bills

MONTH:

COMPANY:

ACCOUNT #: WEBSITE URL:
PHONE#: BILL DUE DATE:

ONLINE ACCOUNT INFORMATION: **USERNAME** **PASSWORD**

BILL TOTAL:

COMPANY:

ACCOUNT #: WEBSITE URL:
PHONE#: BILL DUE DATE:

ONLINE ACCOUNT INFORMATION: **USERNAME** **PASSWORD**

BILL TOTAL:

COMPANY:

ACCOUNT #: WEBSITE URL:
PHONE#: BILL DUE DATE:

ONLINE ACCOUNT INFORMATION: **USERNAME** **PASSWORD**

BILL TOTAL:

NOTES

ONE-TIME Bills

MONTH:

COMPANY:

ACCOUNT #:   WEBSITE URL:

PHONE #:   BILL DUE DATE:

ONLINE ACCOUNT INFORMATION: **USERNAME**   **PASSWORD**

BILL TOTAL:

COMPANY:

ACCOUNT #:   WEBSITE URL:

PHONE #:   BILL DUE DATE:

ONLINE ACCOUNT INFORMATION: **USERNAME**   **PASSWORD**

BILL TOTAL:

COMPANY:

ACCOUNT #:   WEBSITE URL:

PHONE #:   BILL DUE DATE:

ONLINE ACCOUNT INFORMATION: **USERNAME**   **PASSWORD**

BILL TOTAL:

NOTES

WEEKLY EXPENSE *Tracker*

DATES:

DESCRIPTION	CATEGORY	COST	NEED	WANT

DAILY LIFE *Planner*

DATES:

TODAY, *my primary goals are*

MOR

AFT

EVE

TODAY, *my primary goals are*

MOR

AFT

EVE

TODAY, *my primary goals are*

MOR

AFT

EVE

DAILY LIFE *Planner*

DATES:

TODAY, *my primary goals are*

MOR
_____
_____
_____

AFT
_____
_____
_____

EVE
_____
_____
_____

TODAY, *my primary goals are*

MOR
_____
_____
_____

AFT
_____
_____
_____

EVE
_____
_____
_____

TODAY, *my primary goals are*

MOR
_____
_____
_____

AFT
_____
_____
_____

EVE
_____
_____
_____

DAILY LIFE *Planner*

DATES:

TODAY, *my primary goals are*

MOR

AFT

EVE

NOTES:

WEEKLY EXPENSE *Tracker*

DATES:

DESCRIPTION	CATEGORY	COST	NEED	WANT

DAILY LIFE *Planner*

DATES:

TODAY, *my primary goals are*

MOR

AFT

EVE

TODAY, *my primary goals are*

MOR

AFT

EVE

TODAY, *my primary goals are*

MOR

AFT

EVE

DAILY LIFE *Planner*

DATES:

TODAY, *my primary goals are*

| MOR | AFT | EVE |

TODAY, *my primary goals are*

| MOR | AFT | EVE |

TODAY, *my primary goals are*

| MOR | AFT | EVE |

DAILY LIFE *Planner*

DATES:

TODAY, *my primary goals are*

MOR

AFT

EVE

NOTES:

WEEKLY EXPENSE *Tracker*

DATES:

DESCRIPTION	CATEGORY	COST	NEED	WANT

DAILY LIFE *Planner*

DATES:

TODAY, *my primary goals are*

MOR　　　　　　　　　**AFT**　　　　　　　　　**EVE**

....　　...　　...
....　　...　　...
....　　...　　...

TODAY, *my primary goals are*

MOR　　　　　　　　　**AFT**　　　　　　　　　**EVE**

....　　...　　...
....　　...　　...
....　　...　　...

TODAY, *my primary goals are*

MOR　　　　　　　　　**AFT**　　　　　　　　　**EVE**

....　　...　　...
....　　...　　...
....　　...　　...

DAILY LIFE *Planner*

DATES:

TODAY, *my primary goals are*

MOR

AFT

EVE

_____
_____
_____

_____
_____
_____

_____
_____
_____

TODAY, *my primary goals are*

MOR

AFT

EVE

_____
_____
_____

_____
_____
_____

_____
_____
_____

TODAY, *my primary goals are*

MOR

AFT

EVE

_____
_____
_____

_____
_____
_____

_____
_____
_____

DAILY LIFE *Planner*

DATES:

TODAY, *my primary goals are*

MOR

AFT

EVE

NOTES:

WEEKLY EXPENSE *Tracker*

DATES:

DESCRIPTION	CATEGORY	COST	NEED	WANT

DAILY LIFE *Planner*

DATES:

TODAY, *my primary goals are*

MOR
....
....
....

AFT
....
....
....

EVE
....
....
....

TODAY, *my primary goals are*

MOR
....
....
....

AFT
....
....
....

EVE
....
....
....

TODAY, *my primary goals are*

MOR
....
....
....

AFT
....
....
....

EVE
....
....
....

DAILY LIFE *Planner*

DATES:

TODAY, *my primary goals are*

MOR
_____
_____
_____

AFT
_____
_____
_____

EVE
_____
_____
_____

TODAY, *my primary goals are*

MOR
_____
_____
_____

AFT
_____
_____
_____

EVE
_____
_____
_____

TODAY, *my primary goals are*

MOR
_____
_____
_____

AFT
_____
_____
_____

EVE
_____
_____
_____

DAILY LIFE Planner

DATES:

TODAY, *my primary goals are*

MOR

AFT

EVE

NOTES:

FINANCIAL Journal

MONTH 4

Date:_____

INCOME Tracker
- MONTHLY -

SOURCE	AMOUNT	M	T	W	T	F	S	S

ONE-TIME Bills

MONTH:

COMPANY:

ACCOUNT #: WEBSITE URL:
PHONE#: BILL DUE DATE:

ONLINE ACCOUNT INFORMATION: **USERNAME**   **PASSWORD**

BILL TOTAL:

COMPANY:

ACCOUNT #: WEBSITE URL:
PHONE#: BILL DUE DATE:

ONLINE ACCOUNT INFORMATION: **USERNAME**   **PASSWORD**

BILL TOTAL:

COMPANY:

ACCOUNT #: WEBSITE URL:
PHONE#: BILL DUE DATE:

ONLINE ACCOUNT INFORMATION: **USERNAME**   **PASSWORD**

BILL TOTAL:

NOTES

ONE-TIME Bills

MONTH:

COMPANY:

ACCOUNT #:   WEBSITE URL:

PHONE#:   BILL DUE DATE:

ONLINE ACCOUNT INFORMATION: **USERNAME**   **PASSWORD**

BILL TOTAL:

COMPANY:

ACCOUNT #:   WEBSITE URL:

PHONE#:   BILL DUE DATE:

ONLINE ACCOUNT INFORMATION: **USERNAME**   **PASSWORD**

BILL TOTAL:

COMPANY:

ACCOUNT #:   WEBSITE URL:

PHONE#:   BILL DUE DATE:

ONLINE ACCOUNT INFORMATION: **USERNAME**   **PASSWORD**

BILL TOTAL:

NOTES

WEEKLY EXPENSE *Tracker*

DATES:

DESCRIPTION	CATEGORY	COST	NEED	WANT

DAILY LIFE *Planner*

DATES:

TODAY, *my primary goals are*

MOR
_____
_____
_____

AFT
_____
_____
_____

EVE
_____
_____
_____

TODAY, *my primary goals are*

MOR
_____
_____
_____

AFT
_____
_____
_____

EVE
_____
_____
_____

TODAY, *my primary goals are*

MOR
_____
_____
_____

AFT
_____
_____
_____

EVE
_____
_____
_____

DAILY LIFE *Planner*

DATES:

TODAY, *my primary goals are*

MOR

AFT

EVE

TODAY, *my primary goals are*

MOR

AFT

EVE

TODAY, *my primary goals are*

MOR

AFT

EVE

DAILY LIFE *Planner*

DATES:

TODAY, *my primary goals are*

MOR

AFT

EVE

NOTES:

WEEKLY EXPENSE *Tracker*

DATES:

DESCRIPTION	CATEGORY	COST	NEED	WANT

DAILY LIFE *Planner*

DATES:

TODAY, *my primary goals are*

MOR   **AFT**   **EVE**

_____
_____
_____

TODAY, *my primary goals are*

MOR   **AFT**   **EVE**

_____
_____
_____

TODAY, *my primary goals are*

MOR   **AFT**   **EVE**

_____
_____
_____

DAILY LIFE *Planner*

DATES:

TODAY, *my primary goals are*

MOR

AFT

EVE

TODAY, *my primary goals are*

MOR

AFT

EVE

TODAY, *my primary goals are*

MOR

AFT

EVE

DAILY LIFE *Planner*

DATES:

TODAY, *my primary goals are*

MOR

AFT

EVE

NOTES:

WEEKLY EXPENSE *Tracker*

DATES:

DESCRIPTION	CATEGORY	COST	NEED	WANT

DAILY LIFE *Planner*

DATES:

TODAY, *my primary goals are*

| MOR | AFT | EVE |

TODAY, *my primary goals are*

| MOR | AFT | EVE |

TODAY, *my primary goals are*

| MOR | AFT | EVE |

DAILY LIFE *Planner*

DATES:

TODAY, *my primary goals are*

| MOR | AFT | EVE |

TODAY, *my primary goals are*

| MOR | AFT | EVE |

TODAY, *my primary goals are*

| MOR | AFT | EVE |

DAILY LIFE *Planner*

DATES:

TODAY, *my primary goals are*

MOR
....
....
....

AFT
....
....
....

EVE
....
....
....

NOTES:

WEEKLY EXPENSE *Tracker*

DATES:

DESCRIPTION	CATEGORY	COST	NEED	WANT

DAILY LIFE *Planner*

DATES:

TODAY, *my primary goals are*

MOR
....
....
....
....

AFT
....
....
....
....

EVE
....
....
....
....

TODAY, *my primary goals are*

MOR
....
....
....
....

AFT
....
....
....
....

EVE
....
....
....
....

TODAY, *my primary goals are*

MOR
....
....
....
....

AFT
....
....
....
....

EVE
....
....
....
....

DAILY LIFE *Planner*

DATES:

TODAY, *my primary goals are*

- **MOR**
- **AFT**
- **EVE**

TODAY, *my primary goals are*

- **MOR**
- **AFT**
- **EVE**

TODAY, *my primary goals are*

- **MOR**
- **AFT**
- **EVE**

DAILY LIFE *Planner*

DATES:

TODAY, *my primary goals are*

MOR

AFT

EVE

NOTES:

FINANCIAL Journal

MONTH 5

Date:_____

INCOME *Tracker*
- MONTHLY -

SOURCE	AMOUNT	M	T	W	T	F	S	S

ONE-TIME Bills

MONTH:

COMPANY:

ACCOUNT #: WEBSITE URL:
PHONE#: BILL DUE DATE:

ONLINE ACCOUNT INFORMATION: **USERNAME** **PASSWORD**

BILL TOTAL:

COMPANY:

ACCOUNT #: WEBSITE URL:
PHONE#: BILL DUE DATE:

ONLINE ACCOUNT INFORMATION: **USERNAME** **PASSWORD**

BILL TOTAL:

COMPANY:

ACCOUNT #: WEBSITE URL:
PHONE#: BILL DUE DATE:

ONLINE ACCOUNT INFORMATION: **USERNAME** **PASSWORD**

BILL TOTAL:

NOTES

ONE-TIME Bills

MONTH:

COMPANY:

ACCOUNT #:   WEBSITE URL:

PHONE#:   BILL DUE DATE:

ONLINE ACCOUNT INFORMATION: **USERNAME**   **PASSWORD**

BILL TOTAL:

COMPANY:

ACCOUNT #:   WEBSITE URL:

PHONE#:   BILL DUE DATE:

ONLINE ACCOUNT INFORMATION: **USERNAME**   **PASSWORD**

BILL TOTAL:

COMPANY:

ACCOUNT #:   WEBSITE URL:

PHONE#:   BILL DUE DATE:

ONLINE ACCOUNT INFORMATION: **USERNAME**   **PASSWORD**

BILL TOTAL:

NOTES

WEEKLY EXPENSE *Tracker*

DATES:

DESCRIPTION	CATEGORY	COST	NEED	WANT

DAILY LIFE *Planner*

DATES:

TODAY, *my primary goals are*

MOR
_____
_____
_____

AFT
_____
_____
_____

EVE
_____
_____
_____

TODAY, *my primary goals are*

MOR
_____
_____
_____

AFT
_____
_____
_____

EVE
_____
_____
_____

TODAY, *my primary goals are*

MOR
_____
_____
_____

AFT
_____
_____
_____

EVE
_____
_____
_____

DAILY LIFE *Planner*

DATES:

TODAY, *my primary goals are*

MOR

....
....
....

AFT

....
....
....

EVE

....
....
....

TODAY, *my primary goals are*

MOR

....
....
....

AFT

....
....
....

EVE

....
....
....

TODAY, *my primary goals are*

MOR

....
....
....

AFT

....
....
....

EVE

....
....
....

DAILY LIFE *Planner*

DATES:

TODAY, *my primary goals are*

MOR

AFT

EVE

NOTES:

WEEKLY EXPENSE *Tracker*

DATES:

DESCRIPTION	CATEGORY	COST	NEED	WANT

DAILY LIFE *Planner*

DATES:

TODAY, *my primary goals are*

MOR

_____
_____
_____

AFT

_____
_____
_____

EVE

_____
_____
_____

TODAY, *my primary goals are*

MOR

_____
_____
_____

AFT

_____
_____
_____

EVE

_____
_____
_____

TODAY, *my primary goals are*

MOR

_____
_____
_____

AFT

_____
_____
_____

EVE

_____
_____
_____

DAILY LIFE *Planner*

DATES:

TODAY, *my primary goals are*

MOR

AFT

EVE

TODAY, *my primary goals are*

MOR

AFT

EVE

TODAY, *my primary goals are*

MOR

AFT

EVE

DAILY LIFE *Planner*

DATES:

TODAY, *my primary goals are*

MOR

_____
_____
_____

AFT

_____
_____
_____

EVE

_____
_____
_____

NOTES:

WEEKLY EXPENSE *Tracker*

DATES:

DESCRIPTION	CATEGORY	COST	NEED	WANT

DAILY LIFE *Planner*

DATES:

TODAY, *my primary goals are*

- **MOR**
- **AFT**
- **EVE**

TODAY, *my primary goals are*

- **MOR**
- **AFT**
- **EVE**

TODAY, *my primary goals are*

- **MOR**
- **AFT**
- **EVE**

DAILY LIFE *Planner*

DATES:

TODAY, *my primary goals are*

| MOR | AFT | EVE |

_____ _____ _____
_____ _____ _____
_____ _____ _____

TODAY, *my primary goals are*

| MOR | AFT | EVE |

_____ _____ _____
_____ _____ _____
_____ _____ _____

TODAY, *my primary goals are*

| MOR | AFT | EVE |

_____ _____ _____
_____ _____ _____
_____ _____ _____

DAILY LIFE *Planner*

DATES:

TODAY, *my primary goals are*

MOR

AFT

EVE

NOTES:

WEEKLY EXPENSE Tracker

DATES:

DESCRIPTION	CATEGORY	COST	NEED	WANT

DAILY LIFE *Planner*

DATES:

TODAY, *my primary goals are*

- **MOR**
- **AFT**
- **EVE**

TODAY, *my primary goals are*

- **MOR**
- **AFT**
- **EVE**

TODAY, *my primary goals are*

- **MOR**
- **AFT**
- **EVE**

DAILY LIFE *Planner*

DATES:

TODAY, *my primary goals are*

MOR
_____

AFT
_____

EVE
_____

TODAY, *my primary goals are*

MOR
_____

AFT
_____

EVE
_____

TODAY, *my primary goals are*

MOR
_____

AFT
_____

EVE
_____

DAILY LIFE *Planner*

DATES:

TODAY, *my primary goals are*

MOR

AFT

EVE

NOTES:

FINANCIAL *Journal*

MONTH 6

Date:_____

INCOME Tracker
- MONTHLY -

SOURCE	AMOUNT	M	T	W	T	F	S	S

ONE-TIME Bills

MONTH:

COMPANY:

ACCOUNT #:   WEBSITE URL:

PHONE #:   BILL DUE DATE:

ONLINE ACCOUNT INFORMATION: **USERNAME**   **PASSWORD**

BILL TOTAL:

COMPANY:

ACCOUNT #:   WEBSITE URL:

PHONE #:   BILL DUE DATE:

ONLINE ACCOUNT INFORMATION: **USERNAME**   **PASSWORD**

BILL TOTAL:

COMPANY:

ACCOUNT #:   WEBSITE URL:

PHONE #:   BILL DUE DATE:

ONLINE ACCOUNT INFORMATION: **USERNAME**   **PASSWORD**

BILL TOTAL:

NOTES

ONE-TIME Bills

MONTH:

COMPANY:

ACCOUNT #:   WEBSITE URL:

PHONE#:   BILL DUE DATE:

ONLINE ACCOUNT INFORMATION: **USERNAME**   **PASSWORD**

BILL TOTAL:

COMPANY:

ACCOUNT #:   WEBSITE URL:

PHONE#:   BILL DUE DATE:

ONLINE ACCOUNT INFORMATION: **USERNAME**   **PASSWORD**

BILL TOTAL:

COMPANY:

ACCOUNT #:   WEBSITE URL:

PHONE#:   BILL DUE DATE:

ONLINE ACCOUNT INFORMATION: **USERNAME**   **PASSWORD**

BILL TOTAL:

NOTES

WEEKLY EXPENSE *Tracker*

DATES:

DESCRIPTION	CATEGORY	COST	NEED	WANT

DAILY LIFE *Planner*

DATES:

TODAY, *my primary goals are*

MOR
....
....
....
....

AFT
....
....
....
....

EVE
....
....
....
....

TODAY, *my primary goals are*

MOR
....
....
....
....

AFT
....
....
....
....

EVE
....
....
....
....

TODAY, *my primary goals are*

MOR
....
....
....
....

AFT
....
....
....
....

EVE
....
....
....
....

DAILY LIFE *Planner*

DATES:

TODAY, *my primary goals are*

MOR **AFT** **EVE**

TODAY, *my primary goals are*

MOR **AFT** **EVE**

TODAY, *my primary goals are*

MOR **AFT** **EVE**

DAILY LIFE *Planner*

DATES:

TODAY, *my primary goals are*

MOR

AFT

EVE

NOTES:

WEEKLY EXPENSE *Tracker*

DATES:

DESCRIPTION	CATEGORY	COST	NEED	WANT

DAILY LIFE *Planner*

DATES:

TODAY, *my primary goals are*

| MOR | AFT | EVE |

TODAY, *my primary goals are*

| MOR | AFT | EVE |

TODAY, *my primary goals are*

| MOR | AFT | EVE |

DAILY LIFE *Planner*

DATES:

TODAY, *my primary goals are*

MOR

_____
_____
_____

AFT

_____
_____
_____

EVE

_____
_____
_____

TODAY, *my primary goals are*

MOR

_____
_____
_____

AFT

_____
_____
_____

EVE

_____
_____
_____

TODAY, *my primary goals are*

MOR

_____
_____
_____

AFT

_____
_____
_____

EVE

_____
_____
_____

DAILY LIFE *Planner*

DATES:

TODAY, *my primary goals are*

MOR

_____
_____
_____

AFT

_____
_____
_____

EVE

_____
_____
_____

NOTES:

WEEKLY EXPENSE *Tracker*

DATES:

DESCRIPTION	CATEGORY	COST	NEED	WANT

DAILY LIFE *Planner*

DATES:

TODAY, *my primary goals are*

MOR

AFT

EVE

TODAY, *my primary goals are*

MOR

AFT

EVE

TODAY, *my primary goals are*

MOR

AFT

EVE

DAILY LIFE *Planner*

DATES:

TODAY, *my primary goals are*

MOR

_____
_____
_____

AFT

_____
_____
_____

EVE

_____
_____
_____

TODAY, *my primary goals are*

MOR

_____
_____
_____

AFT

_____
_____
_____

EVE

_____
_____
_____

TODAY, *my primary goals are*

MOR

_____
_____
_____

AFT

_____
_____
_____

EVE

_____
_____
_____

DAILY LIFE *Planner*

DATES:

TODAY, *my primary goals are*

MOR

AFT

EVE

NOTES:

WEEKLY EXPENSE *Tracker*

DATES:

DESCRIPTION	CATEGORY	COST	NEED	WANT

DAILY LIFE *Planner*

DATES:

TODAY, *my primary goals are*

- **MOR**
- **AFT**
- **EVE**

TODAY, *my primary goals are*

- **MOR**
- **AFT**
- **EVE**

TODAY, *my primary goals are*

- **MOR**
- **AFT**
- **EVE**

DAILY LIFE *Planner*

DATES:

TODAY, *my primary goals are*

MOR

AFT

EVE

TODAY, *my primary goals are*

MOR

AFT

EVE

TODAY, *my primary goals are*

MOR

AFT

EVE

DAILY LIFE *Planner*

DATES:

TODAY, *my primary goals are*

MOR

AFT

EVE

NOTES:

FINANCIAL *Journal*

www.ingramcontent.com/pod-product-compliance
Lightning Source LLC
Chambersburg PA
CBHW080900170526
45158CB00012B/2863